Five
Chamber
Symphonies

in Full Score

DARIUS MILHAUD

DOVER PUBLICATIONS, INC.
Mineola, New York

Bibliographical Note

This Dover edition, first published in 2001, is a new compilation of five works originally published separately under the group title *Cinq Symphonies pour petit orchestre / Darius Milhaud* by Universal-Edition, 1922. The glossary and lists of contents and instrumentation are newly added.

International Standard Book Number: 0-486-41694-1

Manufactured in the United States of America
Dover Publications, Inc., 31 East 2nd Street, Mineola, N.Y. 11501

CONTENTS

CINQ SYMPHONIES POUR PETIT ORCHESTRE
Five Symphonies for Small Orchestra
[in various instrumentations]

GLOSSARY OF FRENCH TERMS IN THE MUSIC

à, to, at

à peine, barely

allant, moving along

animé, lively, animated

archet, bow *(arco)*

assez lent, rather slow

bouché cuivré, a stopped
   and brassy tone [horn]

calme, calm, gentle

cédez, hold back

chantant, singing

chanté, sung (in a singing manner)

choral, chorale

en dehors, bring out

et (vif), and (quick, brisk)

étude, study

expressif, expressive

grand détaché, played broadly
   with separate bows [string]

joyeux, joyous

lent, slow

mouvement = a tempo

ouverture, overture

prenez la grande Flûte (la petite Flûte),
   take [or change to] flute (piccolo)

rondement, briskly

rude, harsh, rough, impetuous

sans arpeger, without arpeggiating

sans nuancer, without shading

sans ralentir, without slowing down

sautillé mordant, a "bounced" bow
   with a biting edge [string]

sons voilés, veiled (hushed, muted)
   sounds [horn]

sourdine, mute

très expressif, very expressive

très sec, very dry

un peu en dehors, slightly emphasized

violent, forceful, violent

vivement, lively

Footnote, p. 48:

This symphony can be played equally
well by ten strings as in the Léo Sir
double-quintet (that is, high soprano,
soprano, mezzo, alto, contralto, tenor,
baritone, bass, low bass, doublebass).

1ère Symphonie

Le Printemps

Chamber Symphony No. 1: Spring (Op. 43, 1917)

For piccolo, flute, clarinet, oboe, harp
2 violins, viola, cello

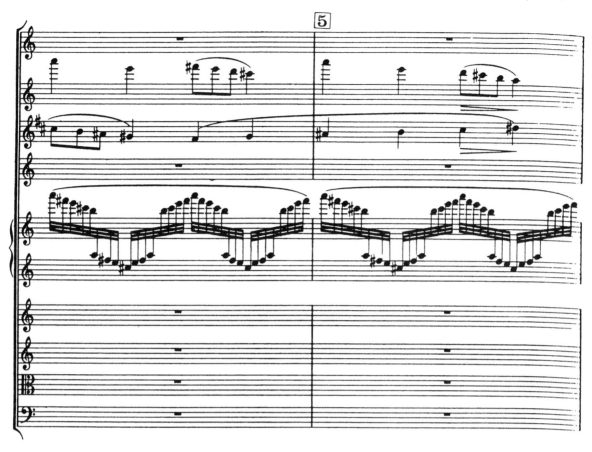

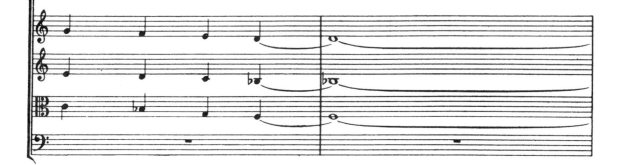

II.

Chantant.

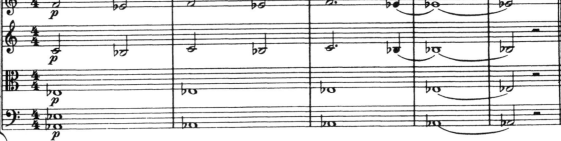

III.

Et Vif!

sans ralentir

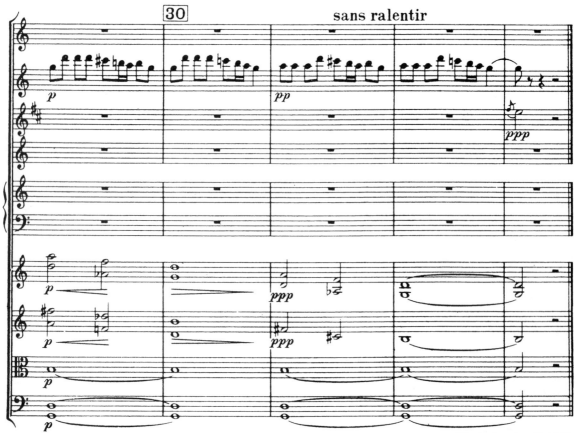

Rio de Janeiro. Mai 1917.

2ᵉ Symphonie

Pastorale

Chamber Symphony No. 2: Pastorale (Op. 49, 1918)

For flute, English horn, bassoon
violin, viola, cello, bass

2ᵉ Symphonie.

(Pastorale.)

Darius Milhaud.
1918.

I.
Joyeux.

II.

Calme.

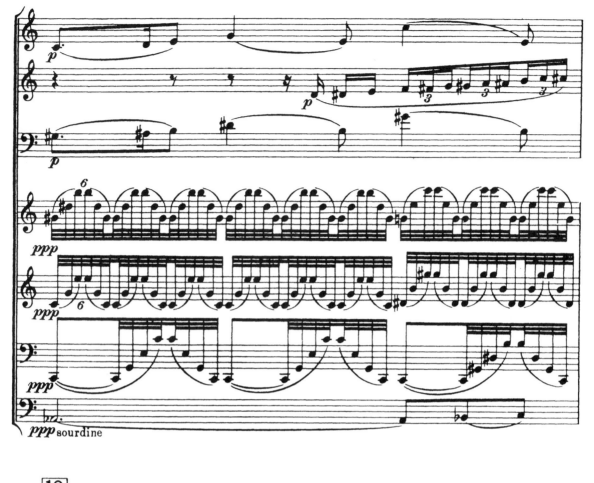

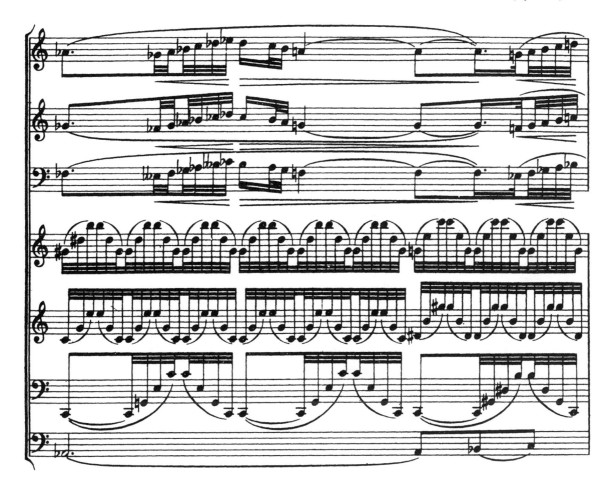

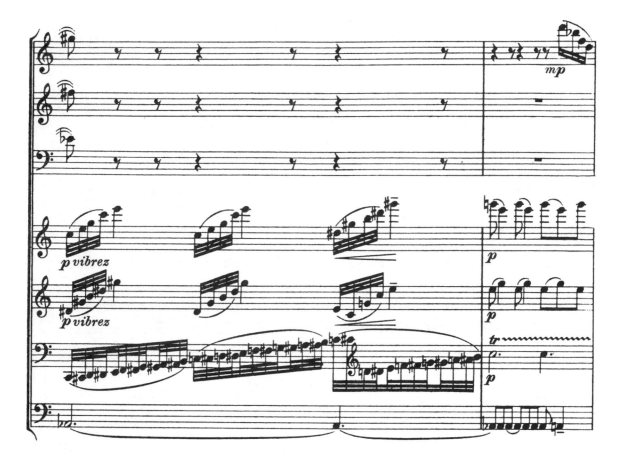

III.
Joyeux.

En Mer Atlantique Sud Décembre 1918.

3e Symphonie

Sérénade

Chamber Symphony No. 3: Serenade (Op. 71, 1921)

For flute, clarinet, bassoon
violin, viola, cello, bass

à Yvonne et Illan de Casa-Fuerte.

3ᵉ Symphonie.

(Sérénade.)

Darius Milhaud.
1921.

II.

III.
Rondement.

30

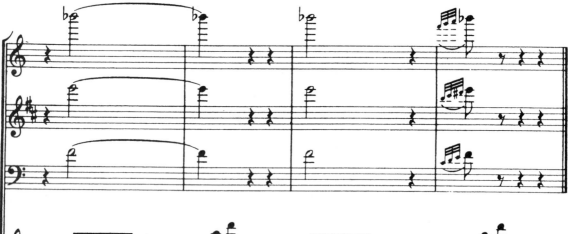

Paris, Juillet 1921.

4ᵉ Symphonie

Dixtuor pour instruments à cordes

Chamber Symphony No. 4: "Tentet" for Strings (Op. 74, 1921)

_____

For 4 violins, 2 violas, 2 cellos, 2 basses

à Madeleine Milhaud

4ᵉ Symphonie.
Dixtuor

pour 10 Instruments à cordes
ou Orchestre à cordes

I. Ouverture.

Darius Milhaud.
1921.

N.B. Cette Symphonie peut également se jouer sur les dix instruments à cordes du double-quintette Léo Sir (c'est à dire Sur-Soprano, Soprano, Mezzo-Soprano, Alto, Contralto, Ténor, Baryton, Basse, Sous-Basse, Contre-Basse).

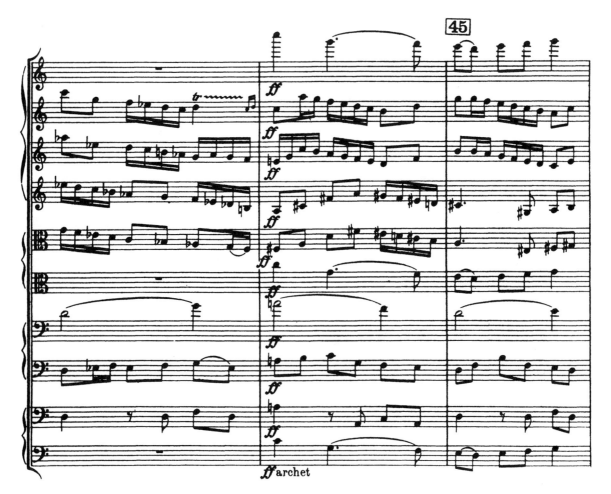

II. Choral.
Assez lent.

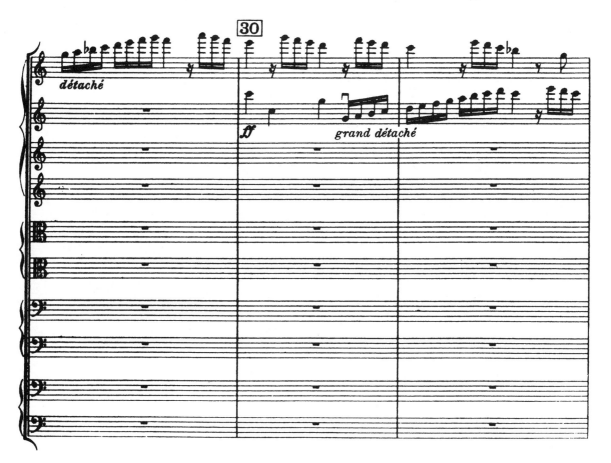

Paris, Septembre 1921.

5ᵉ Symphonie

Dixtuor d'instruments à vent

Chamber Symphony No. 5: "Tentet" for Winds (Op. 75, 1922)

For piccolo, flute, oboe, English horn
clarinet, bass clarinet, 2 bassoons, 2 horns

à Marya Freund

5e Symphonie.
(Dixtuor d'instruments à vent.)

Darius Milhaud.
1922.

II. Lent.

prenez la
petite Flûte

40

III. Violent.
Petite Flûte.

Flûte.

20

Varsovie-Vienne, Fevrier 1922.